Maurizio Fagiolo

with Angela Cipriani

# BERNINI

SCALA

© COPYRIGHT 1981 by SCALA Group S.p.A.
Antella (Florence)
Editor: Angela Cipriani
Design: Maurizio Fagiolo
Layout: Gianfranco Cavaliere
Colour photographs: SCALA group (Angelo
Corsini, Mario Falsini, Mauro Sarri),
except p. 30 (right), Civico Museo di
Bassano del Grappa; p. 31 and 32,
Musei Vaticani (Mario Carrieri); p. 79,
Pubbliaerfoto
Black and white photographs: supplied
by author
Printed by: Amilcare Pizzi S.p.A. -
arti grafiche
Cinisello Balsamo (Milan), 2004

# THE CREATOR OF THE BAROQUE

Giovan Lorenzo Bernini, painter, sculptor, architect, playwright, stage designer and inventor, was born in Naples on December 7, 1598. His mother, Angelica Galante, was Neapolitan, and his sculptor father, Pietro Bernini, was Florentine. Pietro, who had moved to Rome by 1606, taught the young boy to exercise hand and eye continually in his craft. The fundamental basis of young Bernini's artistic training was the concrete experience of his father's workshop (commissioned at the time for work in the Pauline Chapel at S. Maria Maggiore and in S. Andrea della Valle), assiduous study of antique sculpture, and constant drawings from the greatest works of painting and sculpture of the past.

He did his first work during the papacies of Paul V Borghese (1605-1621) and Gregory XV Ludovisi (1621-1623). Rome at the time was a kind of enormous building site, and the leading project was Maderno's addition so St. Peter's. The church was to be the setting of Bernini's work for more than fifty years, as piece by piece he perfected that great edifice. In his youth Giovan Lorenzo worked side by side with his father. There has been considerable discussion about Pietro's and Giovan Lorenzo's respective contributions to several works which, when considered as a group, reveal a progressive distinction of two artistic personalities (they include the sculptures of the Putto with a Dragon, the Putto with a Dolphin, the Faun Wrestling with Cupids, and the recently discovered Four Seasons). Setting aside the flattering exag-

*Self-portrait; c. 1622, Galleria Borghese, Rome.*

gerations of biographers who claim that he did his first work immediately after his arrival in Rome (that is, at less than eight years old), it is true that in the next few years he sculptured busts of Coppola for S. Giovanni dei Fiorentini, Santoni for S. Prassede, Vigevano for S. Maria Sopra Minerva and several others. He restored ancient sculptures (including the Ludovisi Ares and the Borghese Hermaphrodite) for Scipione Borghese, nephew to the pope and an energetic patron, and for Cardinals Ludovisi and Montalto. At the same time he executed "Hellenistic" marble sculptures that demonstrate his great technical skill as well as his profound understanding of the art of antiquity and the Renaissance (The Goat Amalthea, an ornamental sculpture for the Villa Borghese, and St. Lawrence).

In the life-size works he did for Scipione Borghese (Aeneas and Anchises, Pluto and Persephone, Apollo and Daphne, David), he gave an entirely new slant to the relationship between sculpture and observer: the charm of his technical virtuosity leads to a new sense of reality. His portraits, on the other hand, maintained a stern attitude, in keeping with the atmosphere of Paul V's papacy. Bernini's first essay in work combining sculptural and architectural elements was the catafalque for Pope Paul V.

Cardinal Maffeo Barberini was elected pope in 1623 with the name of Urban VIII (1623-1644), and immediately received Bernini in audience.

Baldinucci reports that the pope addressed Bernini with the words, "Great is your good fortune to see Maffeo Barberini pope, but much greater is ours that Cavalier Bernino lives during our papacy". It was a period of serious crisis and conflict for the church-state. While a new wall was being built around Rome, the strength of the Holy Inquisition grew and the Jansenist doctrine spread in opposition to it. The acknowledgement of the Copernican system was celebrated by Maffeo Barberini, but as Urban VIII he condemned it, and forced Galileo to recant while freeing Tommaso Campanella from imprisonment by the Inquisition. Bernini did several portrait busts of the pope, but also sculptured the heads of such adversaries of the pope as Cardinal Richelieu and Charles I of England.

Urban VIII seems to have reacted to the crisis with the unconditional support of the arts, and indeed used patronage as a political weapon. Where Pope Julius II had needed a Michelangelo, Urban VIII now urged his artist friend to prove himself in painting and architecture as well as in sculpture; the sources indicate that Bernini turned to painting chiefly in the first two years of the Barberini papacy. The few canvasses that can be ascribed to him nowadays with certainty reveal a singular, albeit irregular, gift of insight, and a grasp of lessons learnt from Sacchi or Guercino at first and from Rubens and Velásquez later. Bernini's portraits, and he did a great many on canvas as well as in stone, are extraordinary for their synthesis of expression and reflect his parallel efforts in the field of sculpture. Portraiture is at the heart of such varied works as St. Andrew, St. Thomas, and David with the Head of Goliath. But the more "painterly" Bernini's sculpture became, the less he worked with the brush, and he absorbed the coloristic function gradually into modelling form.

In a century in which politics became artifice, it is no surprise that art became politics. Bernini was the minister of this propaganda fide during eight papacies, for almost seventy years, yet he was always driven to create an independent artistic construct. One could say that the Baroque was born at the Barberini court in the meeting of Borromini, Bernini, and Pietro da Cortona. (Among other things, the three of them worked together on the grand building site of

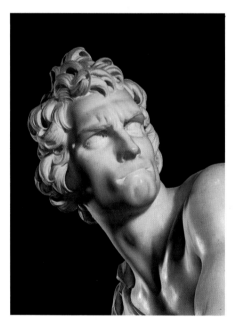

David; detail of the head, c. 1623-1624, Galleria Borghese, Rome.

Palazzo Barberini).

Among the first official appointments Bernini received during Urban VIII's papacy were those of commissario revisore of the conduits of the fountains in Piazza Navona, soprastante of the Castel S. Angelo foundry, and superintendent of the Acqua Felice works. And in 1629, on the death of his father, Bernini became architect of the Acqua Vergine. During these years he designed a great number of fountains in Rome, including the Barcaccia Fountain in Piazza di Spagna (in collaboration with his father), the Triton Fountain in Piazza Barberini, the two Api fountains, the Trevi Fountain, where work was interrupted on the death of the pope, as well as a host of sketches for public and private fountains; in all of these designs there is a sense of allegory together with a sincere love of nature, and a startling mastery of technique that contributes to the illusionist effects.

In this period Bernini, as architect, designed the late-mannerist façade of the Church of S. Bibiana, as well as temporary constructions and settings for sacred occasions (the Canonization of Elizabeth of Portugal, the Catafalque for Carlo Barberini) and profane occasions (the performance of Bernini's plays). He worked also on the Propaganda Fide and the unlucky enterprise of the Campanili for St. Peter's, but undoubtedly his most important work was the solemn and triumphant Baldacchino, that he erected over St. Peter's grave. Together with the decoration of the piers of the crossing, with its niches, loggias and statues, this represents a bold challenge to the work of Michelangelo. As a sculptor he produced the statue of Saint Bibiana as well as vivid figures interacting with the surrounding world (Scipione Borghese, Antonio Cepparelli, Costanza Bonarelli), and the Tomb of Urban VIII, in which he used various different materials in the same work and ranged from the cold austerity of the funeral mask to the liveliness of social conviviality.

The best key to the mind of Bernini, then, would seem to be his sense of theater. His stage settings gave him a chance to try out the most daring architectural effects in an ephemeral context. His craft and skill allowed him to nullify the gap between art and life in the one exceptional form that seemed plausible to a Baroque artist: the post-Copernican form of relativity. A first attempt to bring together all his varied experience was the Raymondi Chapel in S. Pietro in Montorio, the first place in which the total design is Bernini's. The indirect lighting from the side, the white reliefs, and the frescoes on the vault, create what is really a ·spatial setting for the performance of a sacred drama. This is a first attempt at coordinating the various means he was to employ subsequently, with varying nuances, in aiming at an ever more explicit and expressive fusion of the three arts, which he referred to as the mirabile composto, the "beautiful compound". As with the portraits, this achievement is a far cry from the works of his youth. Earlier the action was contained within the gestures of the figures, while now the full effect required the active participation of the observer, a participation which is both psychological and physical. The many works that he created during the first half of the seventeenth century form a complex and highly articulate response to the existential or fideistic doubts that the century of the Baroque gradually revealed beneath the structured certainties of its beginnings.

In 1644 Innocent X Pamphilj (1644-1655) succeeded Urban VIII as pope, and there was an openly avowed purge of the Barberinis and their supporters. The instability of the partially built campaniles at St. Peter's made their demolition advisable, and this provided the excuse for what was virtually a smear campaign against Bernini. Yet the artist does not seem to have been much affected by it. His confidence in his own art found proud and consistent expression in the sculptured marble group of Truth Revealed by Time. The interruption of papal commissions at this period was turned to advantage in the execution of one of Bernini's most unified and consistent works, the Cornaro Chapel in the Church of S. Maria della Vittoria, and his full vindication was not long in coming, in the form of the Four Rivers Fountain in Piazza Navona. One of the most striking of his enterprises (clouded in mystery for centuries) was the periodic "lake" in Piazza Navona, his contribution to the courtyard of the Pamphilj family. The design for this annual setting was based on a theatrical idea of the inventor of the Baroque. In the center of the square stands Mount Ararat surmounted by an obelisk with a dove of peace

*Self-Portrait; c. 1635, Galleria Borghese, Rome.*

on top (after the flood is over). The fountain "lake" beneath is the concrete image of the Biblical event. To complicate the image, there are allegories that also connect the "enigmas" of the obelisk with the flooding of the Nile. This commission was an ideal opportunity for the display of Bernini's happy imagination, the doctrinal subtlety of his emblems, and the reassuring and engaging orthodoxy of his message.

Bernini remained "architect of St. Peter's" even during his period of disgrace, and it was he who designed the marble decoration of the basilica for the jubilee in 1650. It has been estimated that no fewer than two hundred artists worked for him on this project, and this alone of his many undertakings explains the vast influence he inevitably had on contemporary artists, both Italian and non-Italian.

At the conclave in 1655 Alexander VII Chigi became pope. The very day he ascended the papal throne he summoned Bernini to explain his plans for completing the work on St. Peter's. (The pope also turned to Bernini for his family chapel in S. Maria del Popolo). Thus the final aspect of the basilica was conditioned by the layout of the Piazza with Bernini's colonnade, the erection of the Cathedra Petri in the apse, and the Scala Regia connecting the church with the Vatican palaces. And each of these constructions was achieved not in spite of the obstacles represented by pre-existing structures but, paradoxically enough, just because of them. The quadruple colonnade, for example, exploits the slope of the area in front of the basilica and in doing so alters the visible dimensions of Maderno's façade, blending it with Michelangelo's dome, the pagan obelisk, and the Renaissance buildings, and proclaiming the expression of a new sense of urban space.

The buildings Bernini was erecting in Rome at this time (the Church of S. Andrea al Quirinale, the Chigi Palace) had their counterparts in constructions outside the city (the Church of S. Maria dell'Assunzione in Ariccia, the Church of S. Tomaso da Villanova in Castel Gandolfo, and the arsenal in Civitavecchia). In his treatment of the exteriors of his buildings, Bernini tended more and more to define them in terms of their urban function, while emphasizing the theatrical element of surprise in his handling of the interiors. His rules were few and unchanging: simplicity, the fusion of styles, the grandeur of the whole. All of his churches are central-plan structures, but tend towards elliptical forms (from the demolished Chapel of Propaganda Fide to the Bourbon Chapel at Saint-Denis); dynamism takes the place of dogmatic immobility, and the mystical use of space requires a place for a theater audience.

It was during the papacy of Alexander VII that the greatest event in Bernini's life took place, his trip to France to the court of the Sun King to complete the construction of the Louvre. His design with its rusticated base, great colonnade, and balustrade with statues on the top — became the model for much European "princely" architecture. And it was in France, with the portrait bust of King Louis XIV (now at Versailles), that Bernini achieved his most successful sculptural expression of the heroic interpretation of power.

During the papacy of Alexander VII, whom contemporaries referred to as the "pope of great edification" (consciously playing on the double meaning of building and educating), Bernini had many opportunities for building ever more surprising temporary constructions (like the carnival coach for Agostino Chigi, the Catherine wheels for St. Peter's, or the fireworks apparatus in Piazza di Spagna for the birth of the Dauphin of France) and, more importantly, for permanent architectural structures. The pope, who would have liked to rebuild the whole of Rome, turned also to other artists besides Bernini, including Pietro da Cortona (S. Maria della Pace, S. Maria in Via Lata), Borromini (the completion of S. Ivo, the Propaganda Fide, S. Andrea delle Fratte), and Carlo Rainaldi (S. Maria in Campitelli, S. Maria in Montesanto, and S. Maria dei Miracoli in Piazza del Popolo).

Large-scale painting was commissioned for churches and palaces, but painters of the "minor" genres also enjoyed patronage. The classicist theory was extremely influential and found its triumph in Bellori's address in May 1664 at the Accademia di S. Luca, "The Idea of the Painter, the Sculptor and the Architect; and the Choice of Natural Beauties as Superior to Nature". Bernini was so struck by Bellori's address that he followed it faithfully in many of his statements in France.

By the time that Alexander VII died,

Baldacchino, detail; 1624-1633, St. Peter's Rome.

the city's financial resources were so diminished that it was impossible to maintain the same pace of work. Giulio Rospigliosi, who succeeded the Chigi pope as Clement IX (1667-1669), took an interest in Poussin and Claude Lorraine, patronized Maratta, and commissioned Bernini to adorn the S. Angelo Bridge as a kind of monumental Via Crucis leading to St. Peter's. By now Bernini was an old man. He designed the balustrade for the bridge, and the angels, but they were executed by his collaborators, except for two figures which the pope found so beautiful that they were never set up on the bridge itself, where they would have been exposed to the elements, but were replaced by copies.

In 1670 Pope Clement X Altieri (1670-1676) inaugurated a policy of strict economy, in part because of the general discontent with the city's finances. And in the same year the city authorities published a resolution against "Cav. Bernini the instigator of popes to useless expenses in such calamitous times", recommending that his services be dispensed with and that he be left to "make his living with statues". These charges had their effect, for Bernini received no new architectural commissions, and did several works for the Altieri family free of charge — including the Altieri Chapel in S. Francesco a Ripa, the last work in which he expressed himself in his most typical idiom of the "beautiful compound".

Old age, and the repercussions of malicious criticisms of his Louvre project, fostered in him a dramatic concept of life and a religious pietism. The theme of the saving power of prayer, which had already been expressed in the angels for the S. Angelo Bridge, was taken up again in the Bust of Gabriele Fonseca in the Church of S. Lorenzo in Lucina, and in the sculpture of the Blessed Ludovica Albertoni in S. Francesco a Ripa.

Benedetto Odescalchi was already in "the odour of sanctity" when he ascended the papal throne as Innocent XI (1676-1689). His political and moral views were very stern, and so were his ideas about economics. In 1679 he forbade the construction of a "third wing" of the colonnade at St. Peter's; he issued edicts against public immorality, banned theatrical and musical performances, and had the naked figure of Truth on the Tomb of Alexander VII in St. Peter's suitably dressed. In addition to the spiritual crisis of

Bernini's last years, there was the painful experience of a commission set up to determine whether he was responsible for damage to the dome piers of St. Peter's as a result of the work he had done for Pope Urban VIII. Nevertheless, his last works— the altar of the Cappella del SS. Sacramento in St. Peter's and the larger-than-life-size *Salvator Mundi* he carved for Queen Christina of Sweden—are less dramatically "spectacular" and have an almost serene sense of detachment.

Giovan Lorenzo Bernini died on November 28, 1680, and was buried without fanfares in S. Maria Maggiore at two o'clock "in the night", by the light of "only four torches".


A proper reading of Bernini's work requires an exact awareness of his total immersion in his period. Bernini may not be the whole of the Baroque, but he is wholly Baroque. The problems he tried to resolve in his art, from his precocious beginnings to his old age, were the typical problems of the Baroque period. In homage to the principle of metamorphosis, Bernini offered transience where he had found eternity, and he transformed immobility and certainty into movement and ambiguity. And this movement was not merely psychological and representational (as in Borromini, who dramatically expanded and contracted space by treating walls as undulating surfaces); it was actual movement. The statue had ceased to be the ideal: now it was the fountain, the theatrical set, the ephemeral construction.

The synthesis represented by the "beautiful compound" is both absolute and relative. Difficulty is not an obstacle, but rather a stimulus, an opportunity to display a talent that is not merely virtuoso. There is practical difficulty too, as in the case of the Scala Regia, where an unsatisfactory space had to be made rational. And there is artificial difficulty, the delight in inventing a false obstacle to increase the wonder at the result, as in the Four Rivers Fountain, where the obelisk only appears to be supported by a rock that is cleverly fragmented and perforated on the diagonal.

The aim is persuasion. Symbolism and allegory are as intrinsic to Bernini's work as form and technique. Symbolism carries the erudite message, which can be deciphered only by

*Cathedra Petri, detail of Glory; c. 1656-1665, St. Peter's, Rome.*

the cultivated, while allegory, insofar as it is demonstrative, constitutes the real spectacle, theater. The triumphant *agudeza* of the seventeenth century accentuated symbolism and representation to the point at which they verged on caricature — of which Bernini was one of the first to make use, astonishing even the court of France. Bernini did not lose his sense of irony even in the face of death, which, as a practicing Catholic, he contemplated with great serenity. Indeed, in a Counter-Reformation sense, there was something very much alive about his idea of Death. Like Time, Death was characterized by wings and an hourglass — a real being who accompanied man during the brief experience of life, yet was almost too human to evoke the eternal. One has the feeling that the religious crisis of the last years of Bernini's life arose from an awareness of the enduring quality of other values (in this sense, the altar of the Cappella del SS. Sacramento *seems to recall the Holy Sepulchre in Jerusalem*), an awareness that in its disturbing contrasts reminded him of the transience of human life, dramatically present behind the fideistic certainties of a century by this time in total crisis.

By the close of the great period of the Baroque, Baciccio's frescoes in the Church of Gesù and those of Fra Pozzo in S. Ignazio mark the culmination of a long development that was not merely esthetic but affected the whole of society. From this point on, the great experience of Roman Baroque art is to be found outside the city of Rome, in Venice and Genoa, in Austria and Germany, in France and England, in Latin America and even in the Philippine Islands. This art never had much to do with the political importance of the papal state, but was, simply, a marvellous performance that ran for a century under the direction of Bernini, together with Borromini and Barberini, Pietro da Cortona and Pamphilj, Poussin and Chigi. The great artist that was Bernini—stage-designer, actor and director of the vast theatrical spectacular that was Baroque Rome—died as the curtain came down on the show.

NOTE: *The following pages consist of quotations taken from Bernini's contemporaries or from Bernini himself. Bernini's own remarks are printed in capital letters.*

# WORKS AND IDEAS

The Goat Amalthea with the Infant Jupiter and a Satyr; c. 1615, marble h. 45 cm; Galleria Borghese, Rome.

St. Lawrence; c. 1616, marble, 66 x 108 cm.; Contini-Bonaccossi Collection, Florence.

According to Domenico Bernini, when his father was carving St. Lawrence on the gridiron, he put his own leg over the fire and sketched in pencil the expressions of pain on his face and observed the varied effects of his own flesh burned by the fire.

*Aeneas, Anchises and Ascanius; c. 1618-1619, marble, h. 220 cm.; Galleria Borghese, Rome.*

*Pluto and Persephone; c. 1621-1622, marble, h. 255 cm.; Galleria Borghese, Rome.*

WHEN I WAS A YOUTH I OFTEN SKETCHED ANCIENT WORKS. WHENEVER I HAD ANY DOUBTS I WENT TO CONSULT THE ANTINOUS, AS IF IT WERE AN ORACLE. AND DAY BY DAY I SAW IN THAT STATUE BEAUTIES I HAD NOT NOTICED BEFORE AND WOULD NEVER HAVE NOTICED IF I HAD NOT HANDLED A CHISEL. FOR THIS REASON I HAVE ALWAYS ADVISED STUDENTS NOT TO GIVE THEMSELVES UP TO SKETCHING OR MODELLING WITHOUT WORKING [CARVING] AT THE SAME TIME, ALTERNATING CREATION AND IMITATION OR, AS IT WERE, ACTION AND CONTEMPLATION.

*Urban VIII:* "Be careful, Mr. Bernini. This boy is going to surpass you, and without a doubt he will be more skilful than his master".
*Pietro Bernini:* "Your Eminence, remember that in this game the loser wins".

YOU HAVE TO STRUGGLE WITH THE MATERIAL, WHICH IS INTRACTABLE BY NATURE, AND IF YOUR HIGHNESS HAD SEEN THE DAPHNE, YOU WOULD HAVE BEEN ABLE TO SEE THAT THE WORK I DID IN THIS SENSE DID NOT TURN OUT BADLY.

THE ACADEMY SHOULD HAVE PLASTER CASTS OF ALL THE FINEST STATUES, BAS-RELIEFS, AND BUSTS OF ANTIQUITY FOR THE EDUCATION OF THE YOUNG, AND SHOULD HAVE THEM SKETCH THESE MODELS IN ORDER TO CREATE IN THEM AT ONCE AN IDEA OF THE BEAUTIFUL, SOMETHING WHICH WILL SERVE THEM ALL THEIR LIVES. TO SET YOUNG PEOPLE IN FRONT OF REALITY AT THE BEGINNING IS TO LOSE THEM, BECAUSE IN ITSELF THE REAL IS INEFFECTIVE AND MEAN, AND IF YOUNG PEOPLE'S IMAGINATIONS ARE FILLED ONLY WITH THE REAL, THEY WILL NEVER PRODUCE ANYTHING THAT IS BEAUTIFUL OR GREAT.

David; c. 1623-1624, marble, h. 170 cm.; Galleria Borghese, Rome.

Apollo and Daphne; c. 1622-1623, marble, h. 143 cm.; Galleria Borghese, Rome.

ONE SHOULD MAKE LEGS LONG RATHER THAN SHORT, THE SHOULDERS OF MALE FIGURES ALWAYS A BIT BROADER THAN THEY SEEM IN REALITY, AND THE HEADS A BIT SMALLER. IN FEMALE FIGURES, INSTEAD, THE SHOULDERS A BIT NARROW, AND THE FEET SMALL RATHER THAN LARGE.

*« Cavaliere [Bernini] did a portrait sketch of himself in sanguine, using a mirror, for M. Colbert who had requested it »* [Chantelou].

WHEN I WAS YOUNG, ANNIBALE CARRACCI ADVISED ME TO MAKE SKETCHES FROM MICHELANGELO'S LAST JUDGEMENT FOR AT LEAST TWO YEARS, IN ORDER TO UNDERSTAND HOW THE MUSCLES WERE COORDINATED.

*Tomb of Pope Urban VIII; 1628-1647, dark and gilded bronze, white and colored marble; St. Peter's, Rome.*

*With so much life did Bernini render [the great Urban*
*And so impress his soul in the hard [bronze,*
*That he had to set Death himself on [the sepulchre*
*To prove him dead.*
*[Cardinal Rapacciuoli].*

*Triton Fountain; 1642-1643, travertine marble; Piazza Barberini, Rome.*

*Looking across the bridge, he said: « It is a fine sight. I am a very good friend of water, it does my soul good » [Chantelou].*

*Baldacchino; 1624-1633, gilded bronze, wood and marble, h. 28.5 m.; St. Peter's Rome.*

IF OF AN EVENING YOU PUT A CANDLE BEHIND A PERSON SO THAT HIS SHADOW IS THROWN ONTO A WALL, YOU WILL RECOGNIZE THE PERSON FROM THE SHADOW, FOR IT IS A TRUE SAYING THAT NO ONE HAS HIS HEAD ON HIS SHOULDERS IN THE SAME WAY AS ANYONE ELSE, AND THE SAME IS TRUE OF THE REST. THE FIRST THING TO KEEP IN MIND, TO ACHIEVE RESEMBLANCE IN A PORTRAIT, IS THE WHOLE PERSON BEFORE THE DETAILS.

TO SUCCEED WITH A PORTRAIT, YOU MUST FIX AN ATTITUDE AND TRY TO DEPICT IT WELL. THE FINEST MOMENT YOU CAN CHOOSE FOR THE MOUTH IS WHEN THE SITTER STOPS SPEAKING OR WHEN HE STARTS TO SPEAK.

SOMETIMES IN A MARBLE PORTRAIT, IN ORDER TO IMITATE NATURE PROPERLY, YOU HAVE TO DO SOMETHING THAT DOES NOT EXIST IN NATURE. TO RENDER THE DARK COLOR THAT SOME PEOPLE HAVE AROUND THEIR EYES, YOU HAVE TO CUT THE PLACE OF THAT DARKNESS OUT OF THE MARBLE IN ORDER TO CREATE THE EFFECT OF COLOR, AND WITH THIS ARTIFICE MAKE UP FOR THIS DEFECT IN SCULPTURE, WHICH CANNOT OTHERWISE RENDER THE EFFECT.

*Truth; 1646-1652, marble, h. 280 cm.; Galleria Borghese, Rome.*

*Tomb of Sister Maria Raggi; 1642, co-
lored marble and gilded bronze; S. Maria sopra Minerva, Rome.*

THE FIGURE OF TIME CARRY-
ING AND REVEALING TRUTH
IS NOT FINISHED. MY IDEA IS
TO SHOW HIM CARRYING HER
THROUGH THE AIR, AND AT
THE SAME TIME SHOW THE EF-
FECTS OF TIME WASTING AND
CONSUMING EVERYTHING IN
THE END. IN THE MODEL I
HAVE SET COLUMNS, OBELISKS
AND MAUSOLEUMS, AND THESE
THINGS, WHICH ARE SHOWN
OVERWHELMED AND DESTROY-
ED BY TIME, ARE THE VERY
THINGS THAT SUPPORT TIME
IN THE AIR, WITHOUT WHICH
HE COULD NOT FLY EVEN IF
HE HAD WINGS.

*Four Rivers Fountain; 1648-1651, marble and travertine; Piazza Navona, Rome.*

*Model for the Nile (Four Rivers Fountain); terra cotta; Ca' d'Oro, Venice.*

The work had been brought to completion when the Pope decided to go and see it, and inside the fencing and tent covering that still concealed it from the eyes of the public, Innocent made his entry with Cardinal Panzirolo his secretary of state and with fifty of the most intimate members of his court. The sight surpassed the Pope's expectations and exceeded its repute. The Pope walked around it, admiring every part, and then stopped to look at the whole for half an hour; from every side the appearance was majestic. The Pope started to leave twice and twice came back to admire it again. Finally he asked When could he see the waters begin to fall? *Bernini replied intentionally,* Not very soon, because more time was needed to prepare the way, but that he would make every effort to satisfy His Holiness. *Then Innocent gave his benediction and left. But he had not reached the gate of the nearby fence when Bernini, who had artfully and secretly arranged for the water to burst forth from the fountain, gave the signal, and there was a murmur as loud as it was unexpected that left everyone ecstatic with wonder [Domenico Bernini].*

Nor is it the soul that procures the pain of the wound inflicted by its Lord, but a dart in the most tender inner part of its viscera and sometimes even in its heart; and the soul does not know what is the matter nor what it desires. At other times it comes with such impetus and so affects the body that neither feet nor hands can be used; if you are standing, you fall to a sitting position like something that is dropped, for you cannot stand by yourself and can barely breathe. I saw an angel on my left, very beautiful in bodily form, not big but small; the face was bright, just like one of those fine angels that seem to be made of light; I saw a long golden dart in his hands, and it seemed to me that there was a touch of fire on its point. It seemed as if he wounded my heart several times with it and that it penetrated my viscera: and when he drew it out, it was as if he took them away. The pain was so real that I uttered little cries; but the sweetness produced by this intense pain is so great that you wish it would never cease nor ever be without God. It is not a physical pain but a spiritual one, yet it allows the body its part, even too much of it. Jesus, the sweetness is too much: be less sweet or enlarge my heart [St. Theresa of Avila, Libro de su vida].

Cornaro Chapel; c. 1647-1652. Guidobaldo Abbatini, ceiling fresco of the Cornaro Chapel, details of the side walls of the Cornaro Chapel.

Cornaro Chapel, St. Theresa and the Angel; marble; S. Maria della Vittoria, Rome.

*Sala Ducale; 1656-1657, stucco de-
coration of the arch; Vatican Palace,
Rome.*

*Bust of Duke Francesco I d'Este;*
*1650-1651, marble, h. 107 cm.; Mu-*
*seo Estense, Modena.*

*Talking about sculpture and the dif-*
*ficulties encountered in order to suc-*
*ceed, especially in achieving a re-*
*semblance in marble portraits, he told*
*me something remarkable and then*
*repeated it on many occasions; if some-*
*one were to dye his hair, beard,*
*and eyebrows white and, if it were*
*possible, the pupils of his eyes and*
*his lips too, if he then showed him-*
*self in this state even to people who*
*saw him every day, they would barely*
*recognize him. Therefore it is very*
*difficult to achieve a resemblance in*
*a marble portrait, which is all of one*
*color [Chantelou].*

*He no longer wishes to make sculp-*
*ture portraits after paintings, because*
*it is tedious and difficult. He spent*
*fourteen months working on the por-*
*trait of Francesco d'Este [G.B. Rug-*
*geri].*

St. Jerome; 1662-1663, marble, h.
180 cm.; Chigi Chapel, Cathedral, Siena.

Mary Magdalene; 1662-1663, marble,
h. 180 cm. approx., Chigi Chapel, Cathedral, Siena.

MY SON, THIS WORK OF ARCHI-
TECTURE, SANT'ANDREA AL QUI-
RINALE, GIVES ME SOME PART-
ICULAR SATISFACTION DEEP IN
MY HEART, AND AS A RELIEF
FROM MY LABORS I OFTEN
COME HERE TO CONSOLE MY-
SELF WITH MY OWN WORK.

preceding page:
*Colonnade, St. Peter's Square, details;
1656-1667, travertine marble; Rome.*

*Cathedra Petri; c. 1656-1665, colored
marble, bronze, gilded in part, and
stucco; St. Peter's, apse, Rome.*

No one dared write to him about the
cathedra *and the colonnade. When
he thought about them, tears came
to his eyes. He loved his works, and
yet they did not satisfy him and he
was not at all satisfied with them
[Chantelou].*

For St. Peter's Church in Rome [Ber-
nini] recommended two colonnaded
wings so that the façade of the church
would seem taller than it actually was.
He showed me the effect with a pencil and demonstrated that it was the
same relationship as that between
head and arms. He said that architecture consists in a play of propor-
tions taken from the human body
[Chantelou].

*Design for the equestrian statue of Louis XIV; c. 1665-1667, drawing, Museo Civico, Bassano.*

*Equestrian statue of Louis XIV, model; c. 1669-1670, terra cotta, h. 76 cm., Galleria Borghese, Rome.*

*When the king asked him to do his portrait, he replied that this was difficult and would greatly tire His Majesty, since he had to see the model at least twenty times, each time for two hours. It was suggested that [Bernini] do a statue instead of a bust, but he said it would have to be a bust for various reasons.*

*A bust required a concern with details and nuances that was much more engrossing than a statue. The one was made to be kept in a room, the other for a gallery; a bust to be seen nearby, a statue from afar; and, finally, that there was not enough marble even for a bust, much less for a statue [Chantelou].*

*I MUST RETURN TO ROME; I HAD LEAVE ONLY FOR THREE MONTHS AND SOME CHILDREN THAT I CANNOT BRING HERE, THE CATHEDRA PETRI AND THE SQUARE, ARE PRESSING ME TO GO BACK.*

*He said that the Scala Regia was the most daring operation he had ever undertaken, and if he had read about it by someone else, before beginning, he would not have believed it possible [Chantelou].*

ONE SHOULD TRY TO HIDE ARTEFICE AND GIVE THINGS A MORE NATURAL APPEARANCE, BUT IN FRANCE THEY GENERALLY DO THE OPPOSITE.

IF YOU WANT TO SEE WHAT A MAN CAN DO, YOU MUST PUT HIM IN NEED.

HARMONY IS THE MOST BEAUTIFUL THING IN THE WORLD, AND GRANDEUR DOES NOT DEPEND ON THE AMOUNT OF MONEY INVESTED BUT ON THE GRANDEUR OF THE ARCHITECT'S STYLE AND THE NOBILITY OF HIS IDEA.

*Scala Regia; 1663-1666, stucco decorations executed by Ferrata and Naldini; Vatican, Rome.*

I HAVE RECEIVED PERMISSION FROM THE POPE TO WORK TWO OR THREE HOURS ON HOLIDAYS AND SUNDAYS, AS LONG AS THE WORK DOES NOT BECOME FATIGUING.

*He said that he attended to his work with great care, but that there must also be something else, suggesting that it was the grace of God to which he attributed everything [Chantelou].*

*Angel with scroll and crown of thorns; c. 1668-1670, marble; S. Andrea delle Fratte, Rome.*

*Tomb of Alexander VII; 1671-1678, marble and bronze; St. Peter's, Rome.*

*Praying angel, study for the ciborium in the Cappella del Sacramento, terra cotta.*

*Praying Angel, Ciborium of the Cappella del Sacramento, gilded bronze.*

*Ciborium for the Cappella del Sacramento; 1673-1674, gilded bronze and marble; St. Peter's, Rome.*

*Singularis in singulis, in omnibus unicus*
*(from the medal by Cheron, 1674)*

*Bust of Gabriele Fonseca; c. 1668-1673, marble; Fonseca Chapel, San Lorenzo in Lucina, Rome.*

*Blessed Ludovica Albertoni; c. 1671-1674, marble and jasper; San Francesco a Ripa, Rome.*

TO TRY TO RENDER FIGURES EXPRESSIVE I HAVE FOUND ONLY THIS MEANS: TO PUT MYSELF IN THE SAME ATTITUDE THAT I WANT TO GIVE THE FIGURE, AND HAVE MYSELF PORTRAYED BY SOMEONE WHO IS GOOD AT DRAWING.

*Referring to the bust, he said he thought of doing the drapery in such a fashion that it would.resemble heavy silk, but he was not sure whether he would succeed. « In any case », he added, « diligence will make up for what I lack in intelligence » [Chantelou].*

*Then we talked about his works, about David, Persephone and Daphne. M. Ménars repeated Urban VIII's epigram, praised Bernini's works, and declared them superior to those of the ancients. Bernini replied modestly that he owed his reputation to the lucky star that made his contemporaries admire him, but that when he was no longer alive that influence would have no further effect and therefore his reputation would be diminished or decline altogether [Chantelou].*

# THE BAROQUE PERIOD AND ITS THEMES

The life and work of Bernini are summarized in the following pages. His working life is described in seven sections, corresponding to the seven consecutive papacies he served, with attention to his contemporary artists. Eleven sections are devoted to the manifold aspects of Bernini's art and thought in order to illustrate the new impress he gave to Rome, that « city of spectacle » and, in the words of Testi, « that great theater of the world ». Concepts and innovations associated with the name of Bernini are examined in separate sections: dynamism, the feeling for the world of antiquity, metamorphosis, the uses of light, the value of water, and the meaning of fire. Bernini's approach to life and his sense of the vital quality of death are also considered. Each section is thoroughly illustrated in order to evoke the quality of the century that Bernini did so much to transform.

# I. THE « MASTER OF THE WORLD »

For seventy years, under eight successive popes and through continual shifts of domestic and foreign policy, Gian Lorenzo Bernini remained a constant point of reference (and not only a cultural one) at the center of the Catholic world. It was almost as if he created the context in which he lived, rather than being conditioned by it — and indeed, in a document of 1670, he was even accused of being himself « the instigator of popes to undertake useless expense ».

He was the son of a skilled sculptor [1], so that he entered the world of art naturally enough, and rapidly achieved recognition. He was made a *cavaliere* in 1621, when he was only twenty-three years old. About this time he is depicted in a group wearing the chain and court sword of a knight [3] and standing next to one of his first prodigious achievements, the catafalque for Paul V. When Pope Urban VIII made him an official papal artist, Bernini had to concern himself more with painting, architecture, theatrical settings and the organization of clamorous festivities. He offered the pope projects that became ever more and more ambitious. His very face proclaimed his self-assurance. About 1640 he can be seen in a quick self-portrait [7] in the guise of a Spanish-looking cavalier, full of haughtiness and self-importance. His mistress, Costanza Bonarelli, with whom he had some trouble at this period, appears in a lush portrait like a figure out of Rubens [8].

During the pontificate of Innocent X, Bernini's fortunes declined, but the project of the Four Rivers Fountain restored him to almost unlimited power [6]. The Bernini of Grechetto's pompous portrait [9] has all the air of a nobleman, albeit one without feudal possessions. By the time of the visit to France, to judge from another self-portrait [10], he has aged, though his glance is still firm and glowing. But the older Bernini, as seen by his favorite pupil, Baciccio [11], is quite different from the figure in the last known self-portrait (VII, 4). Bernini's role as the right-hand man of many popes suggests an artist who was, perhaps, all too conscious of his own worth. His own mother, remarked that he acted « almost as if he were master of the world ».

1

2

3

4

5

6

1. Bernini (?) *Portrait of Pietro Bernini*, Rome, Accademia di San Luca.
2. Ottavio Leoni, *Portrait of Bernini Wearing the Cross of Knighthood*, 1622.
3.4. Bernini, *Catafalque for Pope Paul V in S. Maria Maggiore*, Giovan Lorenzo with court sword and Pietro Bernini, 1622.
5. *Bernini Presenting Pope Urban VIII with the Plan for the Vatican Loggias*, fresco by Abbatini, 1631. Confessio Petri.
6. *Bernini on a White Horse Inaugurating the Four Rivers Fountain*, painting, detail, Rome, Museo di Roma.
7. Bernini, *Self-Portrait*, c. 1640. Madrid, Prado.
8. Bernini, *Portrait of Costanza Bonarelli*, c. 1635. Florence, Bargello.
9. Grechetto, *Portrait of Bernini*, c. 1633. Genoa, Palazzo Rosso.
10. Bernini, *Self-Portrait*, c. 1665. Windsor Castle.
11. Baciccio, *Portrait of Bernini*, c. 1666. Rome, Galleria Nazionale.

7

8

9

10

11

## II. PREPARATION

Bernini's father, Pietro, worked as a sculptor in Caprarola, Calabria and Naples. He and his family moved to Rome in 1606, when Giovanni Lorenzo was eight years old. The boy learned to work marble alongside his father, and was to be seen even on such important work sites as the Pauline Chapel in S. Maria Maggiore (the family residence was only a few yards away) and the Borghese villa, where sculptured decoration was being carried out. The first reliable source for Bernini's life and work (the biography written by his son Domenico, which preceded Baldinucci's major life) reports that Giovan Lorenzo was extraordinarily precocious, so much so that one is tempted to think that Bernini himself wanted to appear as an *enfant prodige*.

At the beginning of the seventeenth century, Roman sculptors like Maderno, Nicolas Cordier, and Pietro Bernini gave their characters icily rigid features. The bust that Pietro Bernini carved of Antonio Coppola [1] is typical: the portrait was still, as it had been in the world of antiquity, an image for the *penates* (and hence a death image) and was without any living psychological intention.

Nevertheless Pietro Bernini was also a high-spirited and technically very clever sculptor, as can be seen in the large relief with the Virgin of the Assumption, which he did for the Church of S. Maria Maggiore [3], and in the Bacchic sculptural groups he carved with the help of his son [4]. It is no accident that one of the first works that can be documented as Giovan Lorenzo's was at first attributed to Pietro Bernini [2].

Another point of reference is the Tuscan sculptor Francesco Mochi, who was later to work alongside Bernini. The young Bernini of course studied Michelangelo, from whom he derived that passion for the expression of feeling [7] and the dramatic insistence on his own face, as well as the dynamic placing of a sculptural group (what Michelangelo referred to as *contrapposto*). Bernini also studied the classicism of the Carraccis; he was familiar with the work of Caravaggio and the ecstatic vision of Reni, and was interested in Hellenistic sculpture, whose world of « minor » subjects and very high technique was his starting point for a human interpretation of myth.

1

2

4

44

3

5

6

7

1. Pietro Bernini, *Bust of Antonio Coppola,* 1612. Rome, S. Giovanni dei Fiorentini.
2. Bernini, *Putto and Dragon,* c. 1616. New York, private collection.
3. Pietro Bernini, *Assumption of the Virgin* (detail), 1610. Rome, S. Maria Maggiore.
4. Pietro and Giovan Lorenzo (?) Bernini, *Bacchic group* (detail), c. 1615. New York, Metropolitan Museum.
5. Francesco Mochi, *Angel of the Annunciation* (detail), 1603-1608. Orvieto, Museo dell'Opera del Duomo.
6. Pietro Bernini, *St. John the Baptist,* 1615. Rome, S. Andrea della Valle, Barberini Chapel.
7. Bernini, *Damned Soul,* c. 1620. Rome, Palazzo di Spagna.

# III. THE BARBERINI PERIOD

Bernini's real fortune began under Pope Paul V Borghese: Scipione Borghese [2], the open-minded cardinal and nephew of the pope, became Bernini's most important patron, after having been Rubens's protector in Rome. When the young Bernini crossed the threshold of his career, he found an enormous work site in this city. The dominant architects at the time were Maderno and Vasanzio, while Albani, Domenichino, and Guido Reni were the leading painters.

After the short pontificate of the Bolognese Pope Gregory XV (during which Bernini was made *cavaliere* and became a member of the Accademia di San Luca), the long papacy of Urban VIII Barberini [1] began in 1623.

The plague of Urban's twenty-year reign was nepotism. The « handsome pope », as he was called, began by trying to push forward his brothers: the Capuchin Antonio (the only relative who did not exploit his advantages; the inscription on his grave read *His jacet pulvis cinis nihil*) and Carlo, who was made General of the Church (when he died, on the other hand, a statue was set up on the Capitoline, a catafalque was erected, and a memorial monument placed in S. Maria in Aracoeli — all executed by Bernini).

In his youth Maffeo Barberini had written Tuscan, Greek, and Latin verse; some editions of his poetry were illustrated by Bernini [3] as well as by Rubens [4], and he was known for his support of scientists, men of letters, and poets like Marino [6]. It was in Palazzo Barberini that the Baroque style was born. The palace became a microcosm of power with Pietro da Cortona's fresco and works by Bernini and Borromini, as well as a centre for theatrical performances. The archetypal emblem of Baroque art is an architectural work of Bernini's, the *Baldacchino* over the grave of St. Peter [10].

Among Barberini's activities as Pope Urban VIII were the condemnation of astrology (1631), the regulation of witch trials (1635), and of course the trial of Galileo.

Galileo had to make a formal recantation. His theory of « sun spots » was to find a place, however, in a painting in a church in Rome executed by the Tuscan painter Cigoli. [7, 8].

1

2

3

4

5

6

7

8

9

1. Bernini, *Urban VIII,* in an engraving by Mellan, 1631.
2. Rubens (?), *Scipione Borghese,* c. 1630. Rome, private collection.
3.4. *Emblematic frontispieces for two editions of Urban VIII's Poems:* Bernini, *David Slaying the Lion,* 1631. Rubens, *Samson, Lion and Bees,* 1634.
5. *Galileo Galilei,* 1624, drawing by Leoni.
6. *G.B. Marino,* 1624. drawing by Leoni.
7.8. Cigoli, *The Triumph of the Virgin, with the moon showing the «spots» discovered by Galileo,* 1610-1612. Rome, S. Maria Maggiore.
9. Pietro da Cortona, *Project for the Forty Hours of the Sacrament in S. Lorenzo in Damaso,* 1633.
10. Bernini, *Baldacchino in St. Peter's* (first design, with Christ as the Redeemer), c. 1630.
11. Bernini, *Catafalque for Carlo Barberini, in S. Maria in Aracoeli,* plan, 1630.

10    11

# IV. THE PAMPHILJ PERIOD

Giovan Battista Pamphilj's reign as Innocent X lasted a decade. Urban VIII's Francophile policy was at once reversed, because the cardinals elected immediately after the conclave were for the most part pro-Spanish.

The general European situation was complicated by the war in Germany until the Peace of Westphalia (1648), which sanctioned the division of Europe into two blocs. Rome was rocked by these events and lost many of its holdings in Germany. At Christmas 1649 the pope inaugurated the Holy Year, which proved to be a profitable affair, the presence of more than 700,000 pilgrims bringing a considerable amount of money into the depleted papal treasury. (The population of Rome was about 100,000).

In a few short years the pope's strong-willed face made a deep impression on the city; both Velazquez [1] and Bernini [4, 5] did splendid portraits of him. His magnificent palace, enriched by new structures designed by Girolamo Rainaldi, Borromini and Bernini [3, 7] and frescoed by Pietro da Cortona [9], among many others, was further amplified by the virtual inclusion of the entire Piazza Navona as a kind of forecourt.

Borromini's talents had been wasted during the reign of Urban VIII, but his star came into the ascendant now, thanks in part to the support of his patron Virgilio Spada, the pope's secret almoner. Borromini submitted plans for Palazzo Pamphilj (which were rejected), restored S. Giovanni in Laterano for the Jubilee, and directed the work on the Church of S. Agnese from 1652 until 1657. In 1650 he completed work in the Oratorio di S. Filippo Neri, and in 1652 he was invested with the cross of *cavaliere*. His rift with Bernini was by now beyond repair. Bernini called him the « corner cutter » and said he was the architect of «chimeras». Borromini, for his part, was one of those who voted for the demolition of the campanile which Bernini had worked on at St. Peter's, and as soon as he became architect of the Propaganda Fide (1646) tore down the chapel Bernini had built. His grandest project was designed for the pope: a restoration and remodelling of S. Paolo fuori le mura [8], which echoed the work he had done at S. Giovanni in Laterano and at the same time anticipated the ecumenical sweep of Bernini's colonnade at St. Peter's.

1

2

3

4

5

6

V·M·IN PIAZZA NAVONA LA FACCIATA INSINO LA CORNICE CON L'ALZATA della
...mini il frontespizio col timpano ornamento della Cupola e campanili sono Architettura di
Gio Maria Baratta

7

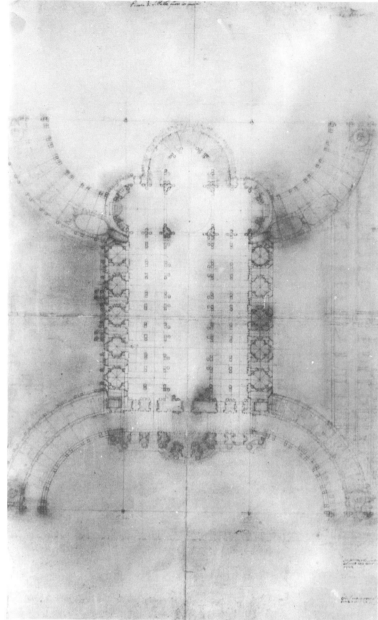

8

1. Diego Velázquez, *Portrait of Innocent X,*
1650. Rome, Galleria Doria Pamphilj.
2. Alessandro Algardi, *Donna Olimpia Pamphilj,* 1649. Roma, Galleria Doria Pamphilj.
3. *Aerial view of Piazza Navona.* On the
left, the Pamphilj complex (Palazzo Pamphilj, the Gallery, and the Church of S.
Agnese).
4. Bernini (?), *Portrait of Innocent X,* c.
1650. Rome, private collection.
5. Bernini, *Innocent X,* c. 1648. Rome, Galleria Doria Pamphilj.
6. *Borromini,* a caricature by Carlo Fontana.
Rome, private collection.
7.8. *Borromini and constructions for the
Pamphilj family:* an unfinished church, *S.
Agnese in Agone,* 1653-1655; a church never
constructed, *plan for the restoration of St.
Paul's outside the walls,* commissioned by
Innocent X.
9. Pietro da Cortona, *fresco in the Galleria
Pamphilj* (architecture by Borromini).

9

# V. THE CHIGI PERIOD

Agostino Chigi, a descendant of the famous Tuscan banker, reigned for twelve years as Pope Alexander VII. The great event of his pontificate was the conversion of Queen Christina of Sweden. She abdicated her throne in 1654 and came to Rome in December 1655, passing through the Porta del Popolo [3, 4], which Bernini adorned for the triumphal occasion.

For the pope whom one source refers to as a « grand edifier » Bernini designed projects on a suitably grand scale. He began work on the colonnaded square in front of the Basilica of St. Peter's, solved the problem of the awkward Scala Regia by turning it into a triumphal entrance to the papal palaces, restored the *Sala Ducale,* and designed the setting for the (doubtful) relic of the *Cathedra Petri.* Pietro da Cortona was another one of the pope's favorite artists. He remodelled S. Maria della Pace [9] in honor of the *pax chigiana* and covered the ceilings of various Roman palaces and churches with enormous paintings [8]. A young Genoese painter, Baciccio [10], started his career with Bernini and was to work alongside his master in some of his most ambitious undertakings.

The pope was also a great promoter of the University, the Sapienza in Rome. Borromini designed the church, the library, and the building façade, with allusions to the heraldic devices in the Chigi crest [6], corresponding to the *Mons Sapientiae,* the « mount of wisdom » [7].

Pietro da Cortona has left an image that summarizes the pope's great building activities: a drawing (engraved by Spierre) [2] shows two artists offering the pope a plan illustrating the mountain in the background; the mountain resembles the mounts in the Chigi crest, and on top of it sits a colossal figure of Alexander the Great. In this allegorical representation, Alexander VII is presented as a greater figure than the hero of antiquity.

Bernini was already at work on a monumental tomb for the pope in 1662; it was unveiled, however, only in 1678. In this monument the figure of death is triumphant, and it is perhaps worth citing in this connection contemporaries who were struck by the pope's intense asceticism: he kept his coffin (designed by Bernini) in his bedroom, and the plates he ate from were ornamented with painted skulls.

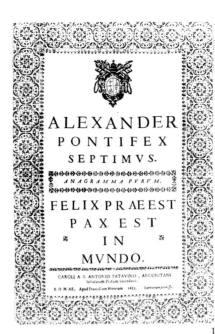

1

2

3

4

5

50

6

7

1. An allegorical *agudeza*. Inaugural anagram for the pontificate of Alexander VII.
2. *Allegory of the « edification » carried out by Pope Alexander VII* (identified here with Alexander the Great and the mythical city on Mt. Athos shown in the form of the Chigi arms), after a drawing by Pietro da Cortona.
3.4. *The Entry in Rome of Queen Christina of Sweden:* Bernini, *Restoration of the Porta del Popolo; the Queen on Horseback.*
5. Bernini, the *Arsenal in Civitavecchia,* drawing by Carlo Fontana, 1655. Rome, private collection.
6.7. *The Mountain of Wisdom and the Chigi mountains:* Borromini, *Plan for the Palazzo della Sapienza,* drawing. Milan, private collection.
Stefano della Bella, engraving for a thesis dedicated to Alexander VII.
8.9. Pietro da Cortona, *painter and architect to the Chigi family:* ceiling fresco, S. Maria in Vallicella, 1660; remodelling of S. Maria della Pace.
10. Baciccio, *Self-Portrait,* c. 1667. Florence, Uffizi.

8

9

10

## VI. THE COURT OF THE « SUN KING »

1

It was the French minister Colbert who summoned the pope's leading artist to Paris. As soon as Bernini crossed the French border, he was received in princely fashion. During his six months' stay, he produced a plan for the Bourbon chapel, a marble bust of the Sun King [7], an altar for the Church of Val-de-Grace, and taught the French the technique of « caricature » [11]; three days before his departure he was present at the laying of the cornerstone of the Louvre [6], but this turned out to be one of his less fortunate enterprises because his plan for the palace was soon abandoned, partly at least owing to the secret jealousy of local architects.

Bernini had already worked on a bust of the great Richelieu [2], whose policies were continued by Mazarin [3], a skillful diplomat of Italian origin. As soon as he arrived in Paris, he burst out with an exclamation that is a program in itself: « Don't speak to me of anything unless it is grand...». Bernini had left his favorite « children » behind in Rome: work was still in progress on *the Cathedra Petri* in St. Peter's [4], on the Scala Regia [5], and the majestic colonnade in St. Peter's Square. He saw Paris, however, as the opposite of the papal city; Rome was a view full of domes and cupolas, while Paris was « like a carding comb » [1]. To his constant companion in France, Sieur de Chantelou (who left a diary of Bernini's state visit), Bernini talked about art and methods, insisted on classicism, and praised Poussin's painting [10].

4

5

The two poles of political and cultural centralization in France were the Louvre and Versailles, the palace in the city (seen as a microcosm of the city) and the royal villa in the country surrounding it. In Bernini's plan for the Louvre [6], the palace stood on rocks, with two figures of Hercules flanking the portal in allusion to the mystical hero who had reached the peak of the « mountain of virtue ». The royal residence at Versailles joined city and park in a cosmic plan, worthy of the « Sun King ».

Although order reigned at the court of France, seeds of doubt were already insinuating themselves: Molière's constantly acid polemical stance, the skeptical pessimism of the great moralists (La Rochefoucauld), and the fables of La Fontaine.

8

9

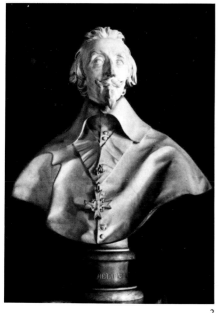

1. Paris, from *Topographia Galliae*, 1650.
2. Bernini (?), *Bust of Cardinal Richelieu*, 1642. Paris, Louvre.
3. Antoine Coysevox, *Cardinal Mazarin*, colored marble. London, private collection.
4. Bernini, *model for the Throne of St. Peter*, terra cotta, 1658-1660. The Detroit Institute of Arts.
5. Bernini (workshop), *model of Constantine*, bronze, c. 1663. Oxford, Asholean Museum.
6. Bernini, *third plan for transforming the Louvre*, engraving, 1665.
7. Bernini, *Bust of Louis XIV*, 1665. Versailles.
8. Bernini (workshop), *Equestrian Statue of Louis XIV*, 1673. Versailles.
9. *Copy from a drawing by Lebrun for the statue of Louis XIV*, Vienna, Albertina.
10. Nicolas Poussin, *Model for the altarpiece of St. Erasmus in St. Peter's* (detail), 1623. Rome, private collection.
11. Bernini, *Caricature of a French cavalier*. Rome, Gabinetto Nazionale delle Stampe.

2

3

6

10

7

11

# VII. THE LAST YEARS

In 1667 Clement I Rospigliosi (once a poet, and a friend of Bernini's at the Barberini court) became pope; he was succeeded by Clement X Altieri [1, 21] — and Bernini lived on into the beginning of Innocent XI's papacy. The tone of the Roman court underwent a profound change at this time. The city suffered badly from the Black Plague and was chronically misgoverned, so that decline was inevitable. There was an almost mystical shift in Bernini's personality now: old age and a number of unsuccessful projects seem to have led him to alter many of the ideas conceived by the « Master of the World ».

During Altieri's reign, Bernini went through a difficult period: shortly after the inauguration of the *Constantine,* his brother Luigi had to flee from Rome as the result of a sodomite assault, and Gian Lorenzo persuaded Christina of Sweden to have the trial suspended. Bernini agreed to work free of charge for the pope's relative, Cardinal Albertoni, and produced the statue of the Blessed Ludovica Albertoni [5] in the throes of death.

During the reign of Innocent XI, Bernini was one of the first to suffer from the pope's moralistic influence. First he had to cover the nakedness of the statue of Truth on Alexander VII's tomb in St. Peter's but worse came with the committee set up in 1680 to check any damage that might have been done to the piers supporting the dome of St. Peter's at the time of Urban VIII. The works Bernini did in these years burn with the ardor of faith — from the arrangement of the *Cappella del SS. Sacramento* [3], originally conceived as a solemn procession, to his last bust of the *Salvator Mundi* [6] for Christina of Sweden. He worked on this until his last days, a gesture of benediction but also perhaps a pathetic farewell. The man who had commemorated the great and powerful of this world, accompanying them to their graves with sumptuous spectacles and splendid « castles of sorrow » (as the catafalques were called), made an almost anonymous exit from life, perhaps at his own request. His bones are mixed with others in the joint tomb [7] of the *nobilis familia Bernini* in S. Maria Maggiore, there to await their resurrection on the very site where Giovan Lorenzo had carved his first marble.

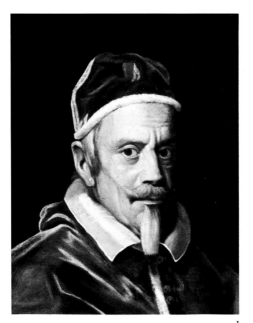

1

2

3

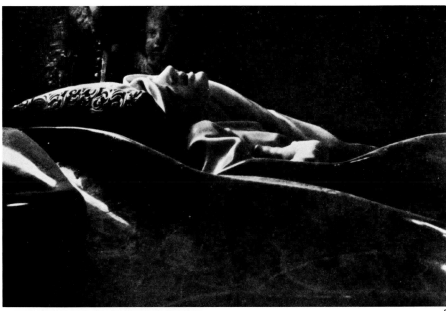

1. Baciccio, *Portrait of Clement X Altieri*, Rome, private collection.
2. Bernini, *Clement X,* drawing, 1675. Liepzig.
3. Bernini, *Plan for the Cappella del Sacramento,* drawing, 1658-1661. Leningrad.
4. Bernini, *Self-Portrait,* drawing, 1675-1680. London, British Museum.
5. Bernini, *Blessed Ludovica Albertoni,* 1671-1674. Rome, S. Francesco a Ripa.
6. Bernini, *Bust of the Salvator Mundi,* 1679-1680. Virginia, Norfolk Museum.
7. Tomb slab of the Bernini family in S. Maria Maggiore.

# VIII. A CITY FOR DISPLAY

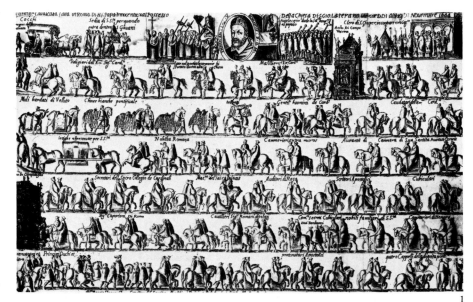

In a city that accommodated one hundred thousand inhabitants, with a further seven hundred thousand pilgrims in jubilee years, it is clear that any artistic undertaking was directed more to the *orbe* than to the *urbe*. Otherwise the vast structures erected, especially in the pontificates of Pamphilj and Chigi, would be inexplicable. And this is the explanation, too, of those enormous festivities that sometimes cost as much as an entire building.

Art as artifice had its assigned place in the field of showmanship, and all the leading artists made their contribution to these entertainments. And then there was the regular theater as well, where the new scenic designers could introduce the discoveries made by sculptors and architects in the creation of dynamic effects, metamorphosis and illusion.

A recurring festivity was the annual Carnival; it was celebrated by the people, but the Church also organized noble dynamic constructions to compete with the noisy festivities in the streets. Bernini designed several allegorical floats, like the one for the Chigi family [6] in which the entire family took part in symbolic costume. The theme of the various spectacles designed to celebrate the Forty Hours of the Sacrament (initiated by Bernini at the Vatican ceremony in 1628) was always sacred, but they were enlivened by sudden theatrical appearances and disappearances, lightning bolts and cloud movements, blinding lights and colourful costumes. One of the most spectacular constructions of this kind was created by Rainaldi for the Church of Gesù [4] in the middle of the century, and took the form of a triumphal pageant.

There were fireworks for religious festivities. Pyrotechnical displays at Castel S. Angelo were unbelievably elaborate, and Bernini himself, according to contemporary sources, made such excessive use of fireworks that part of the lead on the dome of St. Peter's melted. This recurrent firework festival also appeared on the stage [2], and it had its counterpart in the solemn cavalcades on the occasion of the pope taking « possession » of his church [1]. Solemn triumphal arches were erected on these occasions, to provide a theatrical framework for the tangible and rhetorical demonstration of the pope's dominion over the city.

1. *Cavalcade of Innocent X*, engraving, 1644.
2. Giovan Francesco Grimaldi, *Firework display at Castel Sant'Angelo*, 1656.
3. Bernini, *Designs for a carriage for Philip IV of Spain*, Stockholm, National Museum.
4. Carlo Rainaldi, *Project for the Forty Hours of the Sacrament at the Church of Gesù*, 1650.
5. *Orchestra on stage for festivities*, engraving.
6. Bernini, *Carnival float for the Chigi family*, from a painting (Schor?), 1658. Rome, Galleria Nazionale.

4

5

6

# IX. THE ARCHITECTURE OF WONDER

One cannot speak of Bernini strictly as an architect, for he was always an arranger of space rather than a modeller of new forms (as Borromini was). In the case of S. Andrea al Quirinale [1], the entire church has been transformed into a theater, with a stage and a place for the audience: the modern theater, which was born in the church with its sacred performances, here returns to the church again. St. Andrew's martyrdom is depicted in the altar paintings, which show the historical scene. Above it, in the upper part of the lantern, is St. Andrew's vision of God, with the angel host tumbling through the clouds and golden rays of sunlight. Finally there is the ascension of St. Andrew towards the symbolic heaven of the dome.

The catafalques that Bernini designed were in proportion to the boundless spaces of his churches [2]. The architects who followed his lead (e.g., Gherardi [6]), the painters who gave expression to his cosmic ideas (e.g., Baciccio [3]), as well as his more scholarly successors (e.g., Pozzo ([5]), did nothing more than expand Bernini's idea of a totality that would enrich and make more complex the normally accepted function of architecture. Even a remodelling, like Carlo Fontana's design for a church inside the Colosseum [4] (after an idea of Bernini's), became a kind of challenge hurled both at modern artists and at the venerated artists of antiquity.

A striking example of the treatment of interior space is the Cornaro Chapel in S. Maria della Vittoria (cf. XIV, 5). Without the complex mechanics of the architectural treatment, of the treatment of sculpture, painting, *intarsio* and even light, the sculpture of *St. Theresa* would not amount to much. A room in a church has become the perfect counterpart of a theater with stage and stalls for the audience, a place of transition between life and art. You have to walk up and down to feel the credibility of the theater boxes to either side, with the figures of the risen dead leaning over the railing. You have to walk right up to the altar to see the *sancta ex machina,* to see where the light comes from, and to realize that clouds descend and actually are superimposed on the painted and relief scenes.

1

2

1. Bernini, the ceiling in *S. Andrea al Quirinale*.
2. *The crossing in St. Peter's with a catafalque* (photographic superimposition with the catafalque of Pope Alexander VII).
3. Baciccio, *Ceiling of the Church of Gesù*, 1674-1679.
4. Bernini and Carlo Fontana, *Plan for a church inside the Colosseum*, 1675.
5. Fra Pozzo, *Model for the perspective illusionist cupola of the Church of Gesù in Perugia*. Rome, private collection.
6. Antonio Gherardi, *cupola of the Avila Chapel*, 1680. Rome, S. Maria in Trastevere.

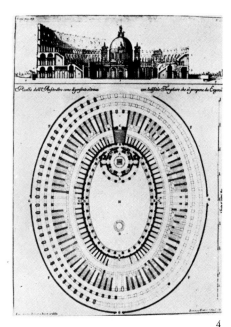

3

4

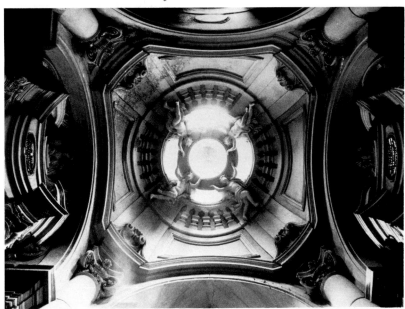

5    6

# X. DYNAMISM

Dynamism was expressed, in sculpture and painting, in the plastic modelling of matter and in the organic modulation of space. The twisted columns of Bernini's *Baldacchino* in St. Peter's (an early symbol of the new style) [2] are closely related to the fluid and liquid manner of a painter like Rubens [1], who was supported in Rome by Cardinal Borghese, one of Bernini's most influential patrons. Bernini could depict the conflict of centripetal and centrifugal forces even in a simple drawing [8], and transform an altar [5] by having the usual altar painting carried by real sculptured angels, as if it were part of a procession or a sudden apparition: the whole complex might perfectly well disappear from one moment to the next, and on the borderline between the fictitious and the possible, he succeeds in making even death something live and active [6]. After all, it was in the seventeenth century that the almost scientific painting technique of *anamorphosis* [3, 4] was developed. When seen at a distance an anamorphic picture creates an impression that is different from the effect at close range, so that the observer has to be active rather than passive: the interpretation of the image is changed simply by moving. This was also the century in which festival floats and constructions [7] were designed to produce striking changes of image before the spectator's very eyes and thereby involve him too in a sense of dynamic movement.

Baroque art was born under the impetus of a new conception of the world. The message of Copernicus was taken up in Rome at once. Copernicus rejected Ptolemaic philosophy and saw the earth as only one element of the cosmos. Then there was the drama of Galileo. And finally there was Newton who brought the intuitive age of the Baroque to its close.

For Bernini, obviously, all these motive forces were fused. The dynamic world and the « new science » found their point of reference in Bernini's habitual territory, the world of spectacle. For the niches in Michelangelo's crossing in St. Peter's, Bernini conceived colossal statues [2] in the attitude of tragic actors. Angels fly aloft bearing the symbols of the Passion, while the giant sculptures below are like actors or singers caught at the highest point of a performance.

1

2

3

4

5

6

1. Peter Paul Rubens, *St. Helen and the Columns of Solomon's Temple,* Grasse, Cathedral.
2. Bernini, *St. Longinus seen through the columns of the Baldacchino,* Rome, St. Peter's.
3.4. An example of anamorphosis: Emmanuel Maignan, *Perspective corridor with St. Francis of Paola and landscape,* 1642. Rome, Convent of Trinità dei Monti.
5. Bernini (workshop), *Angels Bearing the altarpiece, c.* 1657. Rome, S. Maria del Popolo.
6. Bernini, *Memorial of Ippolito Merenda,* 1640-1641. Rome, S. Giacomo alla Lungara.
7. N. Menghini, *Project for the Forty Hours of the Sacrament,* 1640.
8. Bernini, *St. Jerome and the Cross,* 1665. Paris, Louvre.

7

8

# XI. THE MARVELS OF TECHNIQUE

Virtuosity was one of the problems of the seventeenth century, and not only in the visual arts (the word is inevitably associated with music). It was Bernini's childhood contact with his father, Pietro, a man of great skill, that produced his almost istinctive understanding of the secrets of marble [1]. Later, it was his work as a restorer of ancient sculpture [2] that put him in harmony with the technical skill of Hellenistic art, a skill that reached the highest level of imitation. Thus Bernini was able to carve a tear [3] or a virtually transparent leaf [4] and achieve in sculpture almost the same effect as in painting. The school of Bernini, which was active for almost a century, specialized in the study of drapery and the relationship between human flesh and other materials [6], and with this virtuosity astonished the whole of Europe.

But technique can also have what one might call an « engineering » aspect. There was, for instance, an extraordinary festival contrivance in honor of the birth of the Infanta of Spain, featuring the devil in a canebrake, that achieved its effect thanks to a complicated mass of mechanisms and gears. (This production, of 1651, also included a fire-spitting elephant, an exotic device that was revived several years later in the sculpture in Piazza della Minerva [5]). This was a later development of the medieval « automata » but also an indication of the new truth: movement and the technique of transformation as an indication of change in the city itself.

It was Bernini who proposed the synthesis of the arts, harnessing them together in what he called the *bei composto* or the *mirabil composto*. The individual artistic disciplines lose their importance, in so far as they are « means », while the relationship with the observer becomes the « end » of Baroque art. Thus it was possible for there to be a free and casual interchange between techniques, and sculpture could be assimilated into a context that was organized for « rhetoric » and « propaganda ».

But there is something else behind this prodigious and all-embracing pursuit of technical achievement, that reaches out of the field of poetry into the field of science.

1. Pietro and Giovan Lorenzo Bernini (?), *Bacchic group* (detail), c. 1615. New York, Metropolitan Museum.
2. Bernini, *Restoration of the Ludovisi Ares* (detail of the putto), 1621-1623. Rome, Museo Nazionale delle Terme.
3. Bernini, *Pluto and Persephone* (detail of the tears), 1621-1622. Rome, Galleria Borghese.
4. Bernini, *Apollo and Daphne,* (the hands turning into laurel), 1622-1623. Rome, Galleria Borghese.
5. Bernini, *Fireworks for the birth of the Infanta of Spain,* 1651.
6. Bernini (workshop), *Angel with a column,* 1669-1670. Rome, Ponte S. Angelo.

5

6

# XII. THE WORLD
# OF ANTIQUITY

The fundamental problem, and it was not limited to the Baroque, turned out to be, paradoxically enough, the history of the succession of various kinds of classicism. The world of antiquity made two bequests to the seventeenth century: art as imitation and art as idea (two concepts incarnated in painting by Caravaggio and the Carraccis [3]). A sculptor like Bernini seems to adopt both points of view. In his youth he showed his high regard for Hellenistic sculpture in some of his most famous works (the figure of Apollo in his sculpture of Apollo and Daphne is clearly that of the *Apollo Belvedere* [1, 2]), and the idiom he used in France was still imbued with the classical idea. A very important element in his classical orientation was his work in restoring and remodelling ancient sculptures [5].

Bernini's favorite painters included Rubens and Poussin. In Rubens he admired a concept of painting that could be sensational and grandiloquent without rejecting the idea of the classical [4]. In Poussin he loved the moderation and the color. The seventeenth-century Apelles left his finest neoclassic message to the Barberinis (*The Death of Germanicus* [7], unfortunately no longer in Italy), and he is represented in St. Peter's by his *Martyrdom of St. Erasmus*, thanks to Bernini. The leading exponent of the classical idea after the middle of the seventeenth century was Carlo Maratta [8].

The new theory of classicism had its birth in Rome in the writings of Bellori, but it was chiefly in the France of the Sun King that it was put into practice. It was on Colbert's initiative (as well as on the advice of Bernini, who had recently returned from France) that the French Academy was set up in Rome at the Villa Medici: French artists were offered Roman *bon goût,* as a subject for study.

Even in architecture, the practice of restoring old buildings brought about new discoveries and inventions. This was the case both with Bernini [9] and with Borromini, who systematically checked his work against antiquity in search, however, of the neglected detail rather than any codified truth. Almost always Bernini opts for the rule; Borromini chooses the exception.

1

2

3

4

5

6

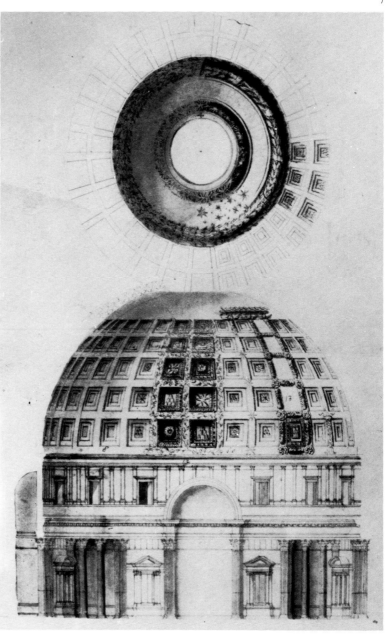

8

1. *The Belvedere Apollo* (detail), Rome, Vatican.
2. Bernini, *Apollo and Daphne* (detail), 1622-1623. Rome, Galleria Borghese.
3 Annibale Carracci, *Fresco in the gallery,* 1597-1600. Rome, Palazzo Farnese.
4. Peter Paul Rubens, *Hermaphrodite,* drawing.
5. Bernini, *Restoration of the Borghese Hermaphrodite* (detail of foot and mattress), 1620. Paris, Louvre.
6 *Antinous,* from Bellori, 1664 (after a drawing by Poussin).
7. Nicolas Poussin, *The Death of Germanicus,* 1627. Minneapolis, Museum.
8. Carlo Maratta, *Self-Portrait,* 1679. Rome, private collection.
9. Bernini and workshop, *plan for the decoration of the dome of the Pantheon,* drawing, c. 1667. Rome, Biblioteca Vaticana.

9

# XIII. METAMORPHOSIS

One of the essential attitudes of the seventeenth century was the new attention that was directed towards nature, and hence to the elements and their transformation; the vision was usually a dynamic one, under the aegis of change and metamorphosis. Once the arts had turned to the subject matter of nature, they also picked up nature's organic rhythms, and even went so far as to suggest a programmatic attitude of « naturalness » (although Bernini has a character in one of his plays remark that « where there is naturalness, there is artifice »).

In Bernini's youthful masterpiece *Apollo and Daphne,* feeling is schematized almost geometrically in ballet form, a calibrated allegory of metamorphosis. The various layers of Bernini's art can be analyzed in this sculpture, and the hidden meaning uncovered; for the episode of Daphne's transformation into Apollo's sacred laurel also stands for « poesy » and hence for Maffeo Barberini (the laurel tree also appears in the Barberini family's coat of arms). The same is true of other youthful works that Bernini did for the Barberinis: *Pluto and Persephone; St. Bibiana;* and the *Baldacchino* in St. Peter's, which ended as a personal monument to the pope. Transformation was also a characteristic feature of another important art form of the period, theatrical representation. In the *commedia dell'arte* (to which Bernini also turned his hand) the text is secondary to plot and gesture, and in the great theatrical revival in Rome the static scene gave way to « visible change ». This tendency is reflected again in Bernini's use of varied materials in the solemn *Cathedra Petri* [2] and in the painted and carved vault of the Cornaro Chapel [4]; in the visible change of an organ into an ideal song of birds sitting on an oak (the emblem of another family, the Chigis) [7]; and in the final, *virtuoso* metamorphosis of architecture into nature (the window sills of the Palazzo Montecitorio [5] transformed into rock).

The great public festivities, with their stunning floats and devices using fire and water, were characteristic of the time. It was here, more subtly than elsewhere, that the world of nature predominated and changed the city [6]. But it was only in the world of the theater [3] that metamorphosis became the sole method.

1

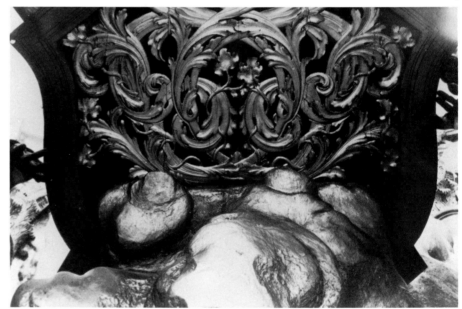

2

3

4

5

1. Bernini, *Apollo and Daphne* (Daphne's foot turns into bark), 1622-1623. Rome, Galleria Borghese.
2. Giovan Paolo Schor, *Cathedra Petri* (between the cloud and the bronze), 1657-1666. Rome, St. Peter's.
3. Bibiena, *Theatrical devices.*
4. Bernini (workshop), *Cornaro Chapel* (ceiling decoration), 1647-1652. Rome, S. Maria della Vittoria.
5. Bernini, *Palazzo di Montecitorio* (detail of a window sill in rock form), 1650-1655. Rome.
6. A. Giorgetti, *Phoebus' chariot, project for the birth of the Infanta of Spain,* 1662.
7. Bernini (workshop), *plan for the organ in S. Maria del Popolo* (transformed into the Chigi oak), c. 1655. Rome, Biblioteca Vaticana.

6    7

# XIV. THE SECRETS OF LIGHT

The question of lighting was vitally important to Bernini's concept of the *bel composto*. The man of the theater used light as a means, without bothering about its mystic sense. In painting the light source was almost always unseen (as in Caravaggio), precisely in order that the figures shown could act as a screen revealing the light. However, where Caravaggio affirmed that the Divinity was the source of light, Bernini, who was bound to a more mundane sense of religion, ended up by admitting that man is the reason for everything, man the center of the world.

Strange to say, Bernini the master of light shunned natural lighting. His hatred of real light was so intense that it became transformed into a kind of willful determination to use natural light in every possible way as if it were artificial light — of which, indeed, Bernini was also a master [4]. There was side lighting, as in the theater. In the Raymondi Chapel [1] and in the chapel with the *Blessed Ludovica Albertoni,* there are windows to the sides of the sculptures. They are invisible to anyone standing in the chapel, and they create an effect of grazing light: not a blaze of light, but an atmosphere in which sacred visions can float. There was also a type of illumination that resembled spotlighting. In the Cornaro Chapel [2, 5] or in the presbytery of S. Andrea al Quirinale, light rains down and alters the color of angels and clouds as they come in contact with its beams. The light does not strike directly but is passed on by sculptured elements, or filtered by the architecture, and the figure of the angel in the *St. Theresa* group glows with the luminosity of a « vision ».

There was also direct or frontal lighting, radiant or from behind (as in the Alaleona Chapel [3]). The greatest triumph came with the *Cathedra Petri* in St. Peter's [6]: here Bernini succeeded in encompassing the exterior space and bringing to the sculpture inside a sense of the infinite, which combines with the real light playing on the sculptured rays and clouds and gives an active, cosmic dimension to the human space so contained. He used a fascinating variety of devices in order to enhance the effect of the « splendor » (as the *Cathedra Petri* is called in documents), and to transmit the single rays into infinite space.

1

2

3

1. Bernini, *Raymondi Chapel* (detail of the side lighting of the altar), 1638-1648. Rome, S. Pietro in Montorio.
2. Bernini, *Plan for the decoration of the Cornaro Chapel*, c. 1647.
3. Bernini, *Alaleona Chapel* (detail of direct lighting of the sculpture *Noli me tangere*), 1649-1650. Rome, SS. Domenico e Sisto.
4. Bernini, *Fireworks plan*, 1661. Leipzig.
5. Bernini, *Cornaro Chapel,* 1647-1652. Rome, S. Maria della Vittoria.
6. Bernini, *Cathedra Petri*, 1657-1666. Rome, St. Peter's.

4

5 6

# XV. THE MEANING OF WATER

The fountain as a subject for art already existed in Naples and Florence (Pietro Bernini's two home cities), but it was Giovan Lorenzo Bernini who transferred the idea from the villa into the city itself, from natural to social space. His fountain sculptures are conceived almost as a function of water, which because of its fluidity and elemental nature became in a way one of the symbolic forms of the Baroque. In the Triton Fountain [1] the sculpture is closely bound up with the factor of water: the Triton sends forth a great jet that originally welled over the shells below and tumbled into the basin with the dolphins. The lily form was a reference to the arms of the French royal family, with whom the Barberinis had connections: Bernini could even create emblems with water.

Bernini produced his finest fountain monument in Piazza Navona around the middle of the century [51]. In the Four Rivers Fountain, he was particularly concerned with the problem of discharging the water and solved this with a sea serpent that swallows it [2] — thus transforming a simple functional element into an active image. Water is thus connected both with the ceremonies of antiquity [3] and with modern hydraulic engineering [4].

Bernini evoked the dynamic aspect of water: in the *Moro* Fountain [6, 7, 8], it is not a banal jet of water that we see but an event in progress. The marine figure has just emerged from the waters on his shell. He has caught a dolphin and is squeezing him between his legs so that the dolphin seems to be spitting out the water in his gullet. The figure portrayed is an actor, and the sculptor seems to have caught the image with a click of the camera. Towards the end of his life, Bernini designed the S. Angelo Bridge [9] as if it were the avenue for a great procession, but once again water entered the image with its liquid vitality: those balustrades [9], with their twisted bronze cords, were created precisely in order to guide the pilgrim in his progress towards St. Peter's, as if he himself were an actor in this great water spectacle. Mature reflection on the Moro carvings so full of life led to the idea behind the Trevi Fountain [10], perhaps the most successful European example of a palace literally transformed into a water display.

1

3

4

5

1.2. Symbol and function. Bernini (workshop), *The Triton Fountain*, 1642-1643. Rome. Bernini, *The Four Rivers Fountain* (detail of the serpent that acts as an outlet for the water), 1651. Rome.
3.4. Classicism and engineering, *Naumachia Domitiani*, from an engraving by G. Lauro. Kircher, *Musical water automa*, from *Musurgia universalis*, 1650.
5. *Allegory*. The lake in Piazza Navona, from a painting by G. P. Panini.
6.8. Bernini (workshop), *stone and bronze model for the Moro Fountain*, Great Britain, private collection.
7. Bernini (workshop), *studies for the Moro*. Rome, private collection.
9. Bernini, *Ponte S. Angelo with balustrades*, 1667-1669.
10. The Trevi Fountain.

6

7

8

9

10

71

# XVI. THE VALUE OF FIRE

Bernini « played » with the elements all his life. The interchange of water and fire became a veritable stage setting in the city, one of continuous transformation. And Bernini brought this interest to the theater too: in a play of 1639, fire is used in a carnival float accompanied by torches. It was one of those entertainments that Bernini organized for families of the Roman nobility. (The use of fire on the stage was common in theatrical performances of the time [2]).

Fire was a triumphal element in ephemeral displays. During the festivities celebrating the Peace of Aachen, organized under the direction of Bernini, there was a programmatic encounter and conflict between water and fire. The two fountains in Piazza Farnese were used as the setting for an arrangement of fireworks, in which a globe of the world was set up with Victory and War kneeling before the Church on top. The allegorical meaning attributed to the event was programmatic: the fire of war was put out by the water of peace.

The image of the cloud was also used in displays involving effects of water and fire, lighting, and the reflections of light, and was also much employed theatrically in apotheoses, and for *ex machina* appearances. Bernini employed it for the first time during the Forty Hours' festivities in 1628, where the lighting was set behind the clouds so that they could alternatively screen the light or allow it to pass.

Fire was a dominant element in public festivities: Carlo Rainaldi used it in Piazza Navona; Menghini used it with cloud effects to transform the whole interior space of a church [5]; Benedetti employed fireworks to create an image of the sun before the public's very eyes, as a symbol of the *Roi Soleil* [6]. The most spectacular display was the one Bernini organized with Schor in Piazza di Spagna [7] to celebrate the birth of the Dauphin of France. It was Cardinal Antonio Barberini who commissioned this *superbissima machina,* and it was he who selected Bernini, according to one source, « because he can take the most irregular and misshapen situation of nature and make it obey the rules and precepts of his rare skill ». He told Bernini to spare no expense and to employ the finest technicians. (Marcello Gondi was put in charge of the fireworks).

1

2

3

1. Bernini, *St. Lawrence*, c. 1616. Florence, Contini-Bonacossi Collection.
2. Alfonso Parigi, *Stage scenery for Bonarelli's Solimano*, 1620.
3. Bernini, *Fireworks project in Piazza Farnese for the Peace of Aachen*, watercolor by Sevin, 1668. Stockholm.
4. Carlo Rainaldi, *Project for Ferdinand IV King of the Romans*, 1653.
5. N. Menghini, *Project for the Forty Hours of the Sacrament*, 1640.
6. Elpido Benedetti, *Fireworks project with the sun appearing*. Celebratory project for the convalescence of Louis XIV, 1687.
7. Bernini and Giovan Paolo Schor, *Festivities for the birth of the Dauphin at Trinità dei Monti*, 1661.

5

6    7

# XVII. THE LIFE OF THE BAROQUE

Seventeenth-century portrait busts reflect not only the new dynamic techniques but (as in the sixteenth century too) the dignity and power of the person depicted. Early in the seventeenth century the theoretician Giovan Battista Agucchi, whose attitude was classical and closely bound up with « idea », had said: « One should not try to discover what the face of Alexander or Caesar was like, but what the face of a king or a magnanimous and powerful warrior should be like ». It was Gian Lorenzo Bernini, in his triumphal bust of Louis XIV, who gave Europe a model for the new fusion of official thought with the new manner of conceiving a posed figure.

In this sense the bust of Thomas Baker [1] and the marble portrait of Charles I of England [5] are masterpieces. The latter work also brings out the political importance that art can have, for Bernini (in accepting a commission to portray a Protestant) was being asked to act not only as sculptor but as quasi-ambassador too. Bernini did a quantity of portaits in marble [2] as well as many portraits in oils [3]. His method of developing a portrait was to start with a character study by way of life drawings [7], or even with modified and « charged » drawings, or caricatures [8]. In the bust of Cardinal Scipione Borghese [9], the figure seems to be in actual conversation with the world around him.

This character almost demands the presence of an observer: as usual, the Baroque work of art is not enclosed within itself but turns outward, towards the interpretation and participation of a hypothetical interlocutor. Scipione Borghese is caught in the act of performing, but the performance would have little sense without some sort of ideal audience. The references to « acting » and « performing » are not incidental: Bernini's aim is always theater. It is worth remarking that Bernini also acted in the plays he wrote, plays written along the lines of the *commedia dell'arte* as depicted by Callot [6]. As Bernini confided to Chantelou during his French visit, he had discovered a new method of catching the pose or gesture of his characters: he assumed the pose himself and then had a student make a sketch.

1

2

3

4

5

1. Bernini, *Portrait of Thomas Baker*, c. 1637-1639. London, Victoria and Albert Museum.
2. Bernini, *Portrait of Urban VIII*, c. 1623. Rome, S. Lorenzo in Fonte.
3. Bernini (?), *Portrait of Poussin* (?), c. 1650, Rome, private collection.
4. Van Dyck, *Portrait of Charles I of England,* London, Buckingham Palace.
5. Bernini, *Portrait of Charles I,* 1636 (destroyed).
6. *Characters from the Commedia dell'Arte,* engravings by Callot.
7.9. Bernini's portraiture methods: *Scipione Borghese,* 1632, in a drawing (New York, Morgan Collection), in a caricature (Rome, Biblioteca Vaticana), and in a bust (Rome, Galleria Borghese)

6

7

8

9

# XVIII. THE VITALITY OF DEATH

It would be a mistake to think that the Baroque concept of «death» was either lugubrious or pessimistic. For a Christian, death is nothing other than the beginning of the true life, and in this sense it is something to be celebrated. Suffice it to mention the countless catafalques that were set up throughout the seventeenth century and the elaborate festivities that accompanied them [6, 7].

Death may appear even in the form of a scientific disquisition [2], but in Bernini's work, it was always bound up with intense spirituality [3]: for him death was an active, living character [5]. This is borne out by the presence of death in its assigned locus, the catafalque. Until Bernini's time the skeleton was a supplementary component [6], but in his work the skeleton took on physical solidity. Death became a star performer.

In early seventeenth-century funerary monuments (like the Cappella Paolina in S. Maria Maggiore, where Pietro Bernini worked, perhaps with the young Giovan Lorenzo) the tomb still functioned as a kind of frozen curtain separating life and death. But Giovan Lorenzo Bernini was to establish a new type of tomb, together with a new reading of death, in the monument he created for Pope Urban VIII in St. Peter's [1, 4].

The key to the whole monument is in the centre, the figure of Death as an apparition. It does not emerge harmoniously from the architectural design; it is something extraneous and hence an active and overwhelming presence. The figure has an open book in its hands and is inscribing Urban's name in gold letters, and one can glimpse the name of an earlier pope on one of the ruffled pages. Yet this is more a figure of Fame than a skeleton: not a source of terror, but a living image — the imposing and necessary complement to human life. Bernini continued to produce new forms of funeral monuments, simpler and yet ever more inventive. The *Tomb of Maria Raggi* in S. Maria sopra Minerva in Rome consists simply of a medallion borne by angels, but it rests on drapery that is both a curtain (separating life and death, as in the tomb of Alexander VII) and, with the Baroque *agudeza,* a transformation of the funeral inscription into a kind of allusive seal of canonization.

2

3

4

1. Bernini, *sketch for Death on the tomb of Urban VIII*, Leipzig.
2. Frontespiece of Errard's book on anatomy, engraving.
3. Bernini, *Sanguis Christi*, engraving by Spierre, c. 1671.
4. Bernini, Tomb of Urban VIII, 1628-1647. Rome, St. Peter's.
5. Bernini, *pavement of the Cornaro Chapel*, Rome, S. Maria della Vittoria.
6. A. Secchi, *Catafalque of the Jesuits*, 1639.
7. Bernini, *Catafalque for the Duke of Beaufort in S. Maria in Aracoeli*, engraving, 1669.

# CONTENTS

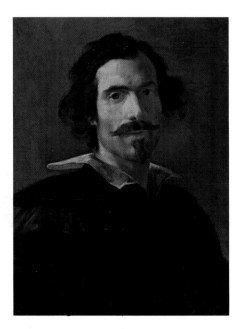

*Self-Portrait; c. 1640, Galleria degli Uffizi, Florence.*